LEARNING A TRADE, PREPARING FOR A CAREER™

THE VO-TECH
TRACK TO SUCCESS IN
ARCHITECTURE
AND CONSTRUCTION

Amie Jane Leavitt

ROSEN
PUBLISHING

Published in 2015 by The Rosen Publishing Group, Inc.
29 East 21st Street, New York, NY 10010

Copyright © 2015 by The Rosen Publishing Group, Inc.

First Edition

Library of Congress Cataloging-in-Publication Data

Leavitt, Amie Jane.
The vo-tech track to success in architecture and construction/Amie Jane Leavitt.—First Edition.
      pages cm—(Learning a trade, preparing for a career)
Includes bibliographical references and index.
ISBN 978-1-4777-7726-8 (library bound)
1. Architecture—Vocational guidance—Juvenile literature. 2. Building—Vocational guidance—Juvenile literature. 3. Industrial technicians—Vocational guidance—Juvenile literature. I. Title.
NA1995.L43 2015
720.23—dc23

                                                        2013051152

Manufactured in the United States of America

CONTENTS

It's a bright Monday morning, and the first school bell has rung for the day. Instead of settling down at their desks with their textbooks in hand, a group of high school students—dressed in jeans, T-shirts, hoodies, and work boots and sporting leather tool belts around their waists—climbs aboard a bus in front of the school.

These students aren't skipping school. They aren't going on a field trip or participating in some mandatory school function either. They are actually part of a program called CTE—or Career Technical Education. CTE gives high school students around the country the opportunity to learn on-the-job trade skills and apply these skills immediately in a real world setting, all while earning high school credits that fulfill graduation requirements.

There are many pathways in the CTE program. Some students get to work as assistants in hospitals. Some get to work on farms and dairies. Others get to work in mechanic shops. Still others get to work in veterinary clinics, graphic arts studios, police stations, hairstyling salons, and firehouses. However, these particular students who just boarded this bus today aren't working in any of these types of industries. Instead, they have chosen to focus their training in the field of architecture and construction. And because of that—for the past

Students in CTE programs get to learn real-world skills in a hands-on way. This particular program in Richmond, California, helps inner-city youth get vocational training while they're still in high school.

eight months since school started—they have been building a house literally from the ground up.

Even though it's early in the morning, each student on the bus today beams with enthusiasm, and they all seem to exude a willingness to share the experiences they've had in the CTE program. Some of the students really enjoyed the concrete projects. Others enjoyed the wall framing, truss installation, and stairway construction. And others have enjoyed every aspect of the project; because of that they hope they will one day become general contractors themselves.

It is clear that this isn't just another group of high school students. Sure, they are young and a little rambunctious on the bus, as most teenagers would be, but they also have clear direction and goals. They have a defined skill set that is being utilized to complete something pretty amazing: a house! Most people do not get the opportunity to learn these types of skills—ever—and here these high school juniors and seniors are not just learning how to do these skills, they are perfecting them.

This is more than obvious when the bus pulls up to the house they have been constructing. It isn't just your run-of-the-mill tract home. It is a beautiful specialty home that because of its excellence in craftsmanship has been slated for a local home tour. It sports five bedrooms, three bathrooms, a full basement, a custom kitchen with handcrafted cabinets and a hardwood floor, and a two-car garage. It's obvious that these students feel a sense of pride in being involved in such a tremendous project. You can tell by the look on their faces that this is an experience that none of them will forget anytime soon.

When asked in an author interview, "What advice would you have for teens who are interested in a profession in the architecture and construction industry?" Ronnie Wiley, landscape designer and construction business owner said, "Get on with some local companies, and don't be afraid to bounce around between a few different ones and even be willing to work for free to start off if nobody wants to pay to train you. If your school offers vocational technology classes then definitely take them!"

Zack Forbush, a lighting contractor, said in an author interview, "If you are looking to be a contractor or working for one, you need to be ready and willing to work hard. I would honestly find a family friend and just ask to tag along a few times to see what a day is like in whatever contracting profession you are interested in."

Finally, Jim Kern, a drafter and engineer, said in an author interview, "Enroll in a vocational/technical college while in high school. An incoming senior at one of the local high schools just finished his associate's degree in drafting and is working as a drafter for a sheet metal fabrication company while completing high school. His goal is to be a mechanical engineer. He will have five years of industry experience by the time he gets his bachelor degree—a huge benefit when potential employers are reviewing job applicants."

Chapter One

"BUILDING" A BRIGHT FUTURE

I n approximately 1,300 high schools and nearly 1,700 two-year colleges around the United States, it's estimated that more than fourteen million students are enrolled in Career Technical Education classes, according to the Career Technical Education Consortium's website. Every state in the union offers some type of CTE coursework. Some states offer courses that align more closely with the economic needs of their area, whereas other states have chosen to align their program to the U.S. Department of Education's (DOE) sixteen career clusters and seventy-nine career pathways. The DOE's clusters include such career fields as health care, education, arts, business, manufacturing, marketing, agriculture, and architecture and construction, among many others.

Previewing a Future Career

College students can also take advantage of CTE courses. Many two-year community colleges offer courses where students can earn an associate of

Since 1996, Ecosa Institute in Prescott, Arizona, has been educating students in architecture and design. Here, Lauren Brulé and Melissa Boo work on the preliminary designs for the Prescott Rodeo Grounds.

applied science (AAS), an associate of arts (AA), or an associate of science (AS) degree. High school students who enroll in high school and college at the same time can earn college credits toward these associate's degrees while still in high school.

CTE programs help students to really experience what work will be like once they graduate from high school should they pursue jobs in these particular industries. They gain practical knowledge that they get to apply on the spot in the actual job. Just like the students mentioned earlier who are building the house for their CTE credits, students in other CTE programs get an opportunity to learn from industry professionals in a hands-on way.

Success in CTE = Success in School

The National Association of State Directors of Career Technical Education Consortium in Silver Spring, Maryland, explains through statistical data how successful this program has been for students:

- Students enrolled in CTE programs have an average high school graduation rate of 90.18 percent.
- More than 70 percent of students concentrating in CTE programs went on to postseondary education after high school graduation, with many completing four-year degree programs.
- Eighty percent of those who have focused on career and technical education classes have met reading and language arts standards on state assessments, and 77 percent have met their mathematics standards on the same state assessments.

Each pathway, or cluster, has numerous types of careers associated with it. The architecture and

Employment in the architecture and construction industry includes high-flying ironworks jobs on skyscrapers, towers, and bridges.

construction cluster is actually organized into three main areas with a variety of career choices in each. These areas are design and pre-construction, construction, and maintenance and operations. The career paths in each area of the cluster provide opportunities for people to design, plan, manage, build, and maintain a variety of structures, including bridges, machinery, homes, sky-scrapers, and commercial buildings. In architecture and

IN THE FIELD: JAMIE COX MARTIN, FORMER CONSTRUCTION FOREMAN

Describe your experience working in the construction industry.

I was a lone woman working with a lot of guys. The first day on the job a guy said, "Are you here to sweep?" I felt I had to prove myself because I was a girl. I eventually got respect because I became the foreman. It was a good experience, and I learned a lot. I did mostly carpentry but have done almost everything: cement, roofing, insulation, sheetrock, siding, framing, ceiling grids, finish carpentry, painting, building new homes, portable classrooms, remodels, signing for deliveries, and forklift operator.

How were you trained for these jobs?

My dad is a general contractor, and I grew up around it—I worked for him a lot. The pay was great! I could work only the summers and focus on school during the year. I also got some cool muscles and great handy skills. I also worked for my county's Building Trades, which is a type of vo-tech program, for nine summers. We would work four ten-hour days.

Describe your experiences as the general contractor for your home.

Negatives: coordinating schedules, getting subs [subcontractors] (framers, cement workers, painters,

continued on page 14

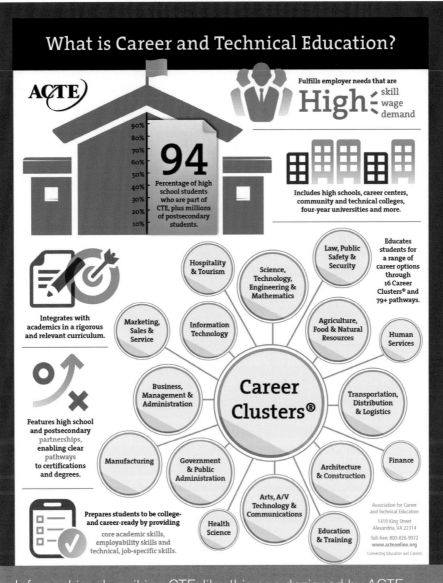

What is Career and Technical Education?

ACTE

Fulfills employer needs that are
High: skill / wage / demand

94 Percentage of high school students who are part of CTE, plus millions of postsecondary students.

Includes high schools, career centers, community and technical colleges, four-year universities and more.

Integrates with academics in a rigorous and relevant curriculum.

Features high school and postsecondary partnerships, enabling clear pathways to certifications and degrees.

Prepares students to be college- and career-ready by providing core academic skills, employability skills and technical, job-specific skills.

Educates students for a range of career options through 16 Career Clusters® and 79+ pathways.

Career Clusters®

- Hospitality & Tourism
- Science, Technology, Engineering & Mathematics
- Law, Public Safety & Security
- Marketing, Sales & Service
- Information Technology
- Agriculture, Food & Natural Resources
- Human Services
- Business, Management & Administration
- Transportation, Distribution & Logistics
- Manufacturing
- Government & Public Administration
- Architecture & Construction
- Finance
- Arts, A/V Technology & Communications
- Health Science
- Education & Training

Association for Career and Technical Education
1410 King Street
Alexandria, VA 22314
Toll-free: 800-826-9972
www.acteonline.org
Connecting Education and Careers

Infographics describing CTE, like this one designed by ACTE (Association for Career and Technical Education), provide helpful facts for young people considering this education route.

continued from page 12

roofers, etc.) to stay on schedule, or show up—I had to fire two subs. It was scary making a million decisions and spending so much money. And all the while, you hope it all turns out well. Getting bids and working with some subs can be very frustrating. It's also difficult sometimes trying to stay on budget and working with the city.

Positives: In the end, we got to have our home exactly the way we wanted it, and we love it! I would have never dared to build my own home had I not had that experience earlier in life as a foreman in the construction industry. Growing up around it definitely made it a lot easier. It was a very stressful seven months, but so worth it!

What advice would you give teens (especially girls) who would like to pursue this profession?

This industry could definitely use more women. Don't let people make you feel like you can't do it. I could do everything a guy could do. It got to the point where the guys would ask for my advice and ask me to show them how it was done.

construction, people work on new structures along with restorations, alterations, and repairs, too.

Careers A-Plenty

Choosing to take classes in the architecture and construction cluster is a wise decision for many reasons.

The first reason is that it's expected that the jobs in this field will increase by about 22 percent in the next decade. The Bureau of Labor Statistics (BLS) recently estimated that there were about nine million jobs in this industry. By the year 2020, the BLS anticipates that there will be more than eleven million architectural and construction jobs in this country.

The second reason is that even if students do not choose to proceed with careers in this industry, taking these classes helps them in many other capacities. It gives them specific skills in a trade that they can use as a side job to work their way through college or to make extra money later on in life, or just to have the confidence and abilities to work on their own personal construction-related projects. These classes give students leadership skills and help them learn how to work as part of a team. They also give the students a great sense of confidence in knowing that they can do challenging things.

Sarah Kendrick is a good example of someone who benefited from taking CTE classes in high school. She took cabinetry courses for three years, from her sophomore to senior years. She started out making basic woodworking pieces like toolboxes and end tables. By her senior year, she was making very advanced pieces that showcased her ability to do excellent craftsmanship.

She made a ten-drawer dresser with attached beveled mirror. She made a china cabinet, a vanity table, several cedar chests, and a smaller five-drawer dresser. All of these items were on display at the end-of-the-year cabinetry show, and it looked like she had enough pieces to nearly fully furnish a house.

In an interview with the author, Kendrick explained, "While I didn't go on to pursue a career in this field, I certainly could have. By the time I graduated, I had the skills and knowledge necessary to work in an advanced cabinetry shop." However, just because she didn't specifically pursue a career in the industry doesn't mean her skills went unused. She has completed numerous home projects since graduating from high school, including making all of the kitchen cabinets in her parents' home and helping on remodeling, recon-struction, and addition projects for more houses as well. "The skills I learned in those classes helped give me confidence. I know how to use power tools. I know how to figure out proper measurements for projects. I am not afraid of trying new things because I know that I tried out many new things in my CTE classes in high school, and I was successful at them."

John Howden is another example of someone who has used his vo-tech classes throughout his life. Howden has been teaching drafting classes

The Sustainable Living Lab in Napa, California, encourages its students to be good stewards of the environment by reusing materials in their construction projects. These students are making planter boxes from the redwood trees that were cut down at their school during a building renovation.

on the high school and college levels for more than thirty years. "When I was in high school, I took all of the drafting classes that were offered. I quickly found that I was very good at drafting and wanted to continue in a career that involved technical design," he explained in an interview with the author. "My teacher was a great influence on my life, and after a volunteer teaching opportunity with my church, I realized I loved teaching, too. So I combined the two. I continue to draw upon what I learned in these early drafting classes as I teach, encourage, and motivate my students today."

Chapter Two

"DESIGNING" YOUR OWN CTE PROGRAM

Often, when you ask high school students what they'd like to do after graduation, they come up with answers that reflect their own environment and the professions they have actually seen in their lives, like doctors, nurses, lawyers, dentists, teachers, or whatever profession their parents are in. While this is not a bad thing, it definitely is limiting. There are thousands of different types of jobs out there that students might be happy doing. But if they don't know about them, they'll never be able to pursue them. That's what is so great about CTE classes. CTE introduces students to a wide variety of occupations in many different industries and helps turn the lightbulb on in their minds to a plethora of possibilities of what they might like to pursue in their own lives.

Meeting with a Guidance Counselor

Students who are considering taking CTE courses should first meet with their high school guidance counselor. This

Guidance counselors provide helpful information to students who are trying to figure out what to do with their futures. Oftentimes, CTE classes are recommended, since they offer hands-on experience in many different fields.

person will be a tremendous help in guiding students toward the pathway that is most suited to them, their interests, their talents, and their future goals.

In addition to working with a guidance counselor, some schools also offer courses that help students find out their strengths and possible interests. These courses, like one offered in the state of Utah, have a series of activities and lessons such as "My Dream," "My Wish List," "The World of Work," and "Occupational Profiles." These allow students to explore, through games and activities, possible skill sets and career options.

Eric Carter, an intern architect who is on his way to becoming a full architect, actually completed one of these types of classes when he was in eighth grade. "I took to heart what I learned in this vo-tech class and really thought about what I wanted to do for a career. I researched the profession of architecture (among several

THE IMPORTANCE OF TECH ED CLASSES: REAL EXPERTS, REAL OPINIONS

Sandon Ellefson, high school cabinetry, woodworking, and house construction teacher: These classes are designed to be more "real world" type classes that will only help students become more creative and successful and better citizens. The students learn that getting what they want will take work, but it is always possible. Tech classes also help to reinforce what students learn in other classes, such as basic math and problem solving. I have had many students who don't get basic math in their math class but they get it in mine simply because it's applied to what they are doing. You can't give students real life skills in other classes or on computers. They need to feel and touch their work.

John Howden, high school drafting teacher: I believe tech ed classes are very important to teach at the high school level because with the demands being placed on colleges and universities to prepare graduates with more advanced coursework, the basic fundamental skills are being left behind or, more tragically, not taught at all. This leaves students with having to know, understand, and complete basic fundamental skills without having been given instruction on the material. On the high school level these essential skills and fundamental information can be taught and covered to give students the necessary knowledge and basic information to be successful in higher-level course work. I relate it to a DuPont commercial, which would advertise: "We don't make the product, we just make it better." High school drafting teachers don't make the engineers and architects; we just prepare them to be better prepared to become engineers and architects because of the basic knowledge gained in high school courses.

other professions) and found that it appealed to many of my interests. That same year, I was also introduced to the work of architect Frank Lloyd Wright. I saw a picture of his famous Falling Water home in Pennsylvania and knew I wanted to go into that line of work," Carter explained in an interview with the author. Later in high school, Carter took classes that related to a career in architecture. "I took two years of drafting classes in high school. These were a great introduction to the basics of drafting. It was beneficial to learn both hand drafting (which is rare these days) and computer-aided drafting. Another benefit was receiving college credit while still in high school, which contributed to my ability to eventually enroll in the University of Utah architecture program a year earlier than I might have been able to do otherwise."

Participate in Work-Study Programs

Many schools have work-based learning programs, internships, or some kind of on-the-job training that high school students can be part of. These opportunities also help inspire students with new career possibilities. Barbara Arrington, a teacher who coordinates the work-based learning program at her high school, explained in an interview with the author, "I currently supervise forty-seven students this semester who are doing paid or unpaid internships as part of their high school credits."

The St. Clair County Technical Education Center in Port Huron, Michigan, offers a variety of CTE classes to its students. Here, these young women work on constructing an architectural model for their drafting course.

These students are pursuing opportunities in all types of industries ranging from health care and education to mechanics and equipment maintenance, welding, drafting, and landscaping. How the program works at this particular high school is that the students go to work a specific amount of hours per week (thirty-five hours total for the semester) during school hours, and then they also attend a class at the high school once every two weeks.

"In this class, we teach the students how to find jobs on the Internet and in the newspaper, how to

Some schools like this one in Denver, Colorado, offer practice interviews for their students. This helps the teens feel more prepared for real interviews when they enter the workforce.

write résumés and cover letters, and how to complete job applications. We also teach them how to work as a team and deal with conflict resolution. In addition, we go through mock interviews, which helps the students practice what it will be like to try and get a job after they graduate," Arrington explained. "Also, every month during lunch time, we have a professional within a specific career come and speak to the students.

IN THE FIELD: JEFF DUVALL, LANDSCAPE DESIGN BUSINESS OWNER

What do you do at your job?

We install sprinklers, sod, plants, retaining walls, paver patios, fire pits and fireplaces, waterfalls, rock walls, and curbing.

Why did you decide to start a landscaping design business?

I started at a sod and landscaping company when I was in high school at age fifteen. After working for this company for about seven years, I decided to start my own landscaping design business. I ran across an ad in the newspaper where a man was selling his equipment, and my wife and I decided to buy it along with a few of his contracts. I went knocking on doors and got a few more commercial accounts. After just one year, we got so busy with all of our contracts that I decided to quit my job and go full time into my own landscaping business.

What skills are most important for this business?

I think it's very important to have good customer service skills. People always make the comment about how nice it must be to have my own business so I can make my own hours and be my own boss. In reality, all my customers are my boss, and they are pretty demanding at times. It takes a lot of patience and drive to work with some people. You have to be willing to work long and hard. It's also important to be organized and be able to keep multiple jobs going all at once. You have to plan ahead and make sure that everything is lined up just right so that things will run smoothly on the job. You also have to be able to handle the accounts payable part of the business. When we get paid from a customer we are immediately on the phone calling our subs and getting invoices so we can get them paid. You also have to know how to work with employees and keep them motivated to keep working. Without our employees we wouldn't be in business. It's important to treat them right.

How did your experiences during high school help you in your career now?

It helped me realize what type of boss I want to be. I learned a lot about sod and how to care for it, which has helped me quite a bit because I can pass that information on to my customers.

What advice would you give teens who would like this career?

Make sure that they really love it or it won't be worth it. At times I wonder why I am in the business and then I sit back and look at some of the projects that we have completed and I'm amazed at what we have been able to create from virtually nothing. It's very rewarding at times, and it's very discouraging at other times. If you don't have a true passion for landscaping and for creating beautiful outdoor living spaces it won't be worth it.

This is open to the entire student body, not just the work-based learning students." In addition, Arrington also makes surprise visits with the students at their job sites to ensure they are really there and doing what they have agreed to do at the job. These work-based learning experiences help students know if they like a particular field and want to pursue it further after high school. "We are teaching our students to prepare for a career, not a job," Arrington clarified. "We encourage all of our students to get further education and training. Many of our students go on to one of the universities in the state, and quite often it is in the field that they interned in."

These work-based learning programs have proven to be very helpful for students as they try to figure out their own personal career paths. As Blake Gneiting, a high school student in the program, explained in an interview with the author, "I have really enjoyed my experience in work-based learning. I work at a landscaping company. I get to work on the equipment and apply some of the skills I have learned in my other classes [e.g., mathematics]. I didn't know much about the job before I started, and now I know more because I have actual experience in the industry. I think if students are interested in work-based learning, they should give it a shot. It will help familiarize them with something new and help them to know if they really like it enough to have a career in it. It will also give them a variety of skills that they can use later on in life, regardless if they go into this profession or not."

Chapter Three

A VARIETY OF JOBS

5

Jobs in the field of architecture and construction are divided into three main clusters: design and pre-construction (architects, computer-aided drafter, landscape designer, etc.); construction (tile setter, carpet installer, framer, roofer, painter, etc.), and maintenance/operations (demolition engineer, highway worker, environmental consultant, etc.). The jobs featured here—and in the interviews throughout the book—will give the reader a sampling of the types of jobs available in this field that can be learned through CTE programs in high school or community college. These entries will help give you an idea of what it's like to work in these professions and what you need to do to pursue and obtain jobs in these industries.

Heavy Equipment Operator

If you've ever driven by a construction site, you've witnessed firsthand the big yellow and orange machines at work. Each of these machines has its own name, but they are collectively called heavy equipment. The

Heavy equipment operators often start out on something small, like this mini excavator. Once they get used to maneuvering these smaller machines, they can get moved up to the larger equipment.

machines—such as front-end loaders, backhoes, track hoes, tractors, dozers, forklifts, and cranes— all have their own duties on the job site and require special skills and coordination to operate. They're definitely not as easy to use (at least at first) as they might look.

Generally, workers start off on the smaller equipment and then, as they gain confidence and experience, move up to larger equipment. Having the ability to work on the large machines definitely gives you an advantage when applying for jobs. "If you're trained on the large track hoes and dozers, you can expect an easier time getting a job and a higher pay rate," explained Sue Robinson, excavator and heavy equipment operator, in an interview with the author.

Most of the training for these machines occurs on the job and can begin while still in high school or even before. Robinson stated, "If you're willing to try out new things and get on the equipment, there are many opportunities for advancement in construction. You will often start out as a laborer in the industry but can soon learn how to run the equipment if you're willing to learn and show some confidence in it."

Plumber

Tradespeople in the plumbing industry learn and utilize a variety of skills, including how to cut pipes and join copper tubing. They also learn how to install water tanks, sewer lines, gas lines, and boilers and how to detect leaks in a plumbing system. Basically, as plumber James Morrison explained in an interview with the author,

Plumbing skills can lead to good high-paying jobs in both residential and commercial projects.

"Plumbing involves anything that flows through a pipe. That includes water, air, sewer, gas, steam, hydraulics, and so forth."

Plumbers can work in a variety of capacities, including in residential homes and commercial buildings. Plumbers can install new plumbing and repair existing systems. They can also help design, plan, and install sprinkling systems for landscaping. Plumbers need to have skills in mathematics—they work with specific formulas in the industry every single day as they figure out system requirements for each project. They also need to be able read blueprints and put those plans into action.

"If you are a plumber, you will always have work," Morrison explained. "If your power goes out, you can light a candle. But if your water stops flowing through your water pipes or your sewer system has a problem, you can't just let that go. Plumbers are needed in just about every aspect of our world today."

Plumbing courses are available in many high school CTE programs, and follow-up training is available in apprenticeships and community college classes.

Welder

Welders work with metal, alloys, and composite materials. They cut, shape, and combine materials to make different parts for the architecture and construction industry and the automotive, engineering, and aerospace industries, too. There's even a need for welders in hyperbaric environments. That means welding in areas of high pressure, usually underwater. This can be dangerous, but also very well-paid and quite interesting work. In order to do this type of welding, though, you must be a certified scuba diver and have extensive training, which can take up to two years.

Thomas Byram, a pipe fitter, welder, and steam fitter, learned the welding trade while he was in high school and then furthered his skills in the United States Marine Corps. His advice to teens is to start

In the welding industry, protective clothing is required, including a helmet with face mask, safety glasses, leather coats, aprons, and heavy insulated gloves.

young. "The younger you start, the earlier you can retire. Also, be prepared to travel for work. Sometimes the jobs aren't exactly where you live, so if you have flexibility in where you will work, you will have more opportunities and better pay rates."

Other welders agree with Byram. "Take as many welding classes as you can in high school," said one welder. "Study hard in your other classes too like science and mathematics. Welding really is a science and you have to know why and how it works if you want to be good at it. And, mathematics—especially geometry and trigonometry —is used all the time in welding."

Electrician

Just like plumbers must go through years of training to be qualified for their profession, so must an electrician.

Licensing varies by state but most often includes such levels as apprentice electrician, journeyman electrician, residential journeyman electrician, master electrician, and residential master electrician. Each type requires a set number of hours of training, education, and experience. And after that, the electrician must pass the official state exam to be licensed on that level.

High school students interested in becoming an electrician should take some classes in the basics to learn how to install wiring, fuses, and other components related to an electrical system. They should also learn about the science of electricity and how and why it flows. Math skills are highly important for electricians. They do calculations all the time to figure out current draws and the geometrical and special needs of a project. One of the best ways for teens to find out if they are interested in this profession is to job shadow to see if it's something they really want to do.

Architectural Woodworker

An architectural woodworker is a high-end woodworker, someone who has really mastered the basics of carpentry and cabinetry and can make beautiful pieces out of wood. This trade allows a person to add natural beauty to buildings with such things as specialty stair rails, columns, ceiling work, and panels. "In this profession, you must be very creative," says Robert Rask. "You also must have an in-depth knowledge of how wood works in various conditions like temperature and humidity."

Rask recommends that high school students who are interested in this profession start taking

Using power equipment like this drill is commonplace in CTE classes. As this teen demonstrates, proper safety gear is always a must.

as many woodworking classes as possible. "Get to know the equipment and what it's like to work with different types of wood," he explains. "Start out with small projects and then move forward from there. I would highly recommend that after high school, students take CTE classes in woodworking in college and even apprentice in a cabinetry shop. The more experience you get in this trade, the better you will be at it."

IN THE FIELD: CASSY SMOOT DICKERSON, INTERIOR DESIGNER

Why did you go into interior designing?

I wasn't sure what I wanted to major in at first. I took a bunch of classes in different areas of interest to see what I would like. When I took an intro to interior design class, I knew it was something I liked and would be good at. I stuck with it and even got a talent award scholarship toward my tuition. Once I selected my major and got into the program I really enjoyed learning about all aspects of interior design. I was even able to take some interesting electives like color theory, furniture design, a reupholstery class, floral design, and a woodworking class where I designed and built a desk. My internship at a local design firm was probably one of my most helpful things I did while in school.

Did you take any classes in high school that prepared you for this?

In high school there was one course offered in interior design, and I took it and loved it. I also took art classes, too. I wish I would have taken some drafting classes, but at the time, unfortunately, I thought those were only for boys.

What is it like to be an interior designer?

Most of my work experience is in "commercial" interior design. Right out of school I got a job at the university I attended. They have an in-house planning department and have designers, architects, land-scapers that take care of carpentry, reupholstery, and other things regarding physical facilities. About 80 percent of my time was spent working on the computer specifying furniture and creating furniture layouts. I also spent a lot of time meeting or commu-nicating with clients and reps from the furniture, carpet, and fabric industry. I really liked how we used design to help solve problems and make life easier and more pleasing for people. Where I live, there is a huge hospitality market, and they have in-house designers for all the major hotels and casinos and home builders for model homes. There is also a huge furniture mart in town. There are so many areas to work in, even health care design. There are lots of options in interior design!

What skills would help a person be successful in this job?

People skills, problem solving, ability to multitask, time management, attention to detail, rendering, drafting, color theory, lighting, textiles, and be famil-iar with products and budgets.

What advice would you have for a high school student interested in this career?

Try it out, see if you can intern or assist a designer or work with a vendor. People were really nice to me as a student and willing to help. It can feel a little

continued on page 40

continued from page 39

more "competitive" once you are out in the field, but there are nice people everywhere (as well as some superficial snobs, but don't let them bother you!). Read magazines and blogs. There are tons of things you can do. Don't worry about your own personal style, learn as much as you can about different styles and your own will develop over time.

Architect

According to Eric Carter, intern architect, early in their careers, "architects tend to do a lot of drafting to get an understanding of how building systems come together. They also complete a variety of tasks including building code research, preparing presentation materials, and building models (either physical or digital). More experienced architects manage projects, present proposals for new projects, and design the buildings through a combination of hand sketching and digital formats."

Like every profession, there are pros and cons. One con of the job, according to the architects interviewed for this book, seems to be the long hours (oftentimes fifty hours or more per week and sometimes all-nighters) that are required when project deadlines are looming. One pro is the reward of seeing something you've designed actually completed. Another pro is the ever-changing nature of the work. "No two days are alike," explains architectural designer Charley Danner in an interview with the author. "Often, a day may start with a coordination

The tools in architecture are much different than the tools for welding, plumbing, or heavy equipment operating. An architect uses a drafting table, tracing paper, a compass, triangles, scales, and computers in his or her daily arsenal.

meeting with the design team (architects, engineers, contracts, and owners). It may then be filled with making changes to the design following the meeting, usually taking markups or hand sketches and incorporating them into the computer software. A lunch hour may be spent learning about a new building product or updates to the building code. There may be an early afternoon meeting to do final coordination with a project manager and architect before sending revised designs to the client. On a good day, you are out of the office by 5:30 PM."

A person who would be most successful and happy in the field of architecture is one who thrives under pressure, can work as part of a team, can maintain a balance of work and personal life, and has a creative, artistic eye.

High school students interested in this profession should take math classes (particularly calculus), art classes, physics classes, 3D modeling classes, and drafting classes. "Practice observational sketching," recommends Danner. "Think of sketching as analyzing what you are drawing rather than just re-creating an image and you will be ahead of the game." Danner also recommends, "High school students should plan on five years of additional education at an accredited university following high school graduation. In addition, they should be familiar with the licensing processes for their own states."

Chapter Four

I'M OUT OF HIGH SCHOOL, NOW WHAT?

igh school graduation can be both an exciting time and an uneasy time. Throughout all of your life up to this point your decisions have basically been made for you. You went to school and did your homework (hopefully!), and that was really the extent of your duties. But what happens now that you're out of school? The world is open to you—like a big buffet with so many options—and you have to figure out what route is best for you!

That is where CTE courses are particularly helpful. Students who have taken technical education classes at least have an idea of what they could possibly do to make a living. They have some specific skills that can help them get started in the workforce right away without having to wait for years to obtain a college degree. Now, that's not to say that CTE students do not go on to further their education. Many do. However, those who do choose that route are often able to use their trade skills to work their way through college in meaningful, well-paid positions.

43

Many students who enroll in CTE classes not only finish high school but also go on to attend colleges and universities.

Apprenticeships: Learning on the Job

One way that high school graduates can move forward in their trades is by becoming an apprentice. That's the path that James Morrison of California took. Morrison grew up in the world of plumbing. His father was a plumber, and some of his older brothers had also gotten into the industry as adults. After high school, Morrison decided to choose this profession for his career. He wanted to be a unionized plumber. In California, in order to become a plumber with a union, a person has to complete five years of apprenticeship. "The union set that all up for me," Morrison explains. "They got me a full-time forty-hour-per-week job with one of their union companies and then helped me know what courses I had to take in night school, which ended up being two nights a week for three and a half hours each night for five years." Once Morrison finished his apprenticeship and his required schooling, he was ready to take the state plumbing test. When he passed it, he became a journeyman plumber. "Being a plumber with a union definitely has its advantages," Morrison states. "You get full benefits and a pension, which is something you probably won't get as a non-union plumber."

Morrison explains that in plumbing, a journeyman is the first level. From there the next levels up are foreman, general foreman, superintendent, estimator, etc. With each level comes more responsibility and thus a higher pay rate, too. Currently, Morrison is a foreman and is in charge of eleven other workers. "There's always room to grow as a plumber," Morrison explains. "If you are capable enough in the industry and prove yourself on the job, you'll be able to move up the ladder."

CTE Classes in College

Another option to further your trade skills, or obtain trade skills, after high school is to enroll in CTE classes in college. Most two-year community colleges offer these types of classes, and within two years or

less you could have both a college degree (associate's degree) and the necessary training and certificates to let you jump immediately into the workforce. Many of these classes are taught in a hands-on way, too. For example, if you're in a cabinetry class, you will spend

Building and installing trusses is a highly skilled part of a project. The students here at Moraine Park Technical College built this small home as part of their semester project.

a lot of your time in the woodworking shop working with power tools and other equipment as you make furniture, cabinets, and other similar items. If you're in a surveying class, it's a pretty good guess that you'll spend a significant amount of time out in the field with surveying equipment learning in a real world setting. Of course, you'll have some class-work, too, but the purpose of CTE is to really get people out in the field and learning through experience.

Guidance counselors are available to students in college just like they are in high school. Go meet with one. Come prepared to ask questions and to really listen to their answers. Talk to them about what your interests are and ask for their advice. They have likely heard it all before from many other students and will be able to give you some good tips. Ask them about work-study programs. Ask them about apprenticeships. Have them assist you in putting together a schedule that will help meet your short- and long-term goals. If you're concerned about how you'll pay for college, guidance coun-selors can help with that, too. Many scholarships and grants are available in this industry, and some companies will even pay for you to go to school while you work for them.

A Chat with Experts

It is also wise to talk to people in the actual pro-fession that you are considering going into. Ask if you can job shadow with them for a day or so. You might think that you want to be a carpenter, for example, but what you have painted in your mind of that profession could be very different from what it actually is. It is absolutely crucial to see what the job is like before you

When this young woman job shadowed a local architect for the day, she spent part of her time looking over blueprints for the project.

get too invested in it. High school senior Blake Gneiting explained, "That's why I really like getting high school credit in the work-based learning program. I get to work in an industry and explore new doors to see if I really like it before I get too invested into it as an adult."

Once you do decide to pursue a particular profession, it's really wise to find someone to be your mentor. A mentor is someone who already works in the field who can give you tips and advice on how best to proceed forward. This person can also be a good resource for you later on when you try to find a job. He or she will have contacts in the industry for one. And second, this person can also give you advice as to how to properly build your résumé, what kinds of certifications to get, and what kinds of skills are most needed in the industry.

While James Morrison had to complete a formal apprenticeship in order to become a unionized plumber, many other people learn on the job in what can be

At the Trade Institute of Pittsburgh, this instructor guides a student who is learning basic skills in masonry.

dubbed "informal" apprenticeships. For example, in an interview with the author, Dallas Calderwood explained that when he graduated from high school, he mentioned to a friend that he would be interested in a job in the construction industry. His friend made that happen by getting him a job framing houses. He was able to get paid to learn as he worked. Since Calderwood was eager to learn and was a dedicated hard worker, he was successful at breaking into this profession. He also had some experience in the industry, which helped him, too. "In high school," he explained, "I took shop classes and did my best at learning geometry. This helped because while framing you run into a lot of drops and different angles that can become difficult unless you have a little bit of math know-how. Drafting classes are a great thing as well because it is always a bonus with the bosses when you can read blueprints and help them solve problems that might arise. It's good job security."

Proving Competency

Morrison found that in plumbing he was required to demonstrate a certain level of competency in order to be a certified plumber in his state. He had to finish an apprenticeship and pass a state test. This might sound like just another hoop that a worker has to jump through, but it is really quite important that states require this. After all, you certainly wouldn't want some random person off the street without any specific training to come into your home and install electrical wires. That could lead to a very dangerous situation.

IN THE FIELD: JIM KERN, AEROSPACE AND ASTROSPACE DRAFTER AND ENGINEER

What made you want to go into drafting?

I had been working as a commercial truck driver and was hurt on the job. I could not work in that industry and needed to find a new career. I had always been interested in mechanical design. Drafting seemed to be a good entry point into that industry.

What was your job like in the aerospace and astrospace industry?

Upon graduating with my associates of science degrees in design and drafting engineering technology and architectural drafting, I was hired by Boeing Commercial Airplane Company, in Washington State, as a tool design/drafter. I designed tooling and drafted the fabrication drawings for Boeing 737, 757, 767 commercial jetliners and worked on the wings of the B-2 Bomber. After Boeing I worked at Douglas Aircraft Company in California as a tool design engineer. I designed the master tooling that defined the transition between the cockpit and the fuselage. I also worked on the design of the T-45 Goshawk Fighter Training aircraft. At DuPont Advanced Composites in Delaware I worked on satellite structures and the robotic arm for the Space Shuttle but also ventured into design of specialty military and sporting goods products such as an enhanced helmet

continued on page 54

continued from page 53

for the special forces and a tri-spoke carbon/graphite bicycle wheel for triathlon racers.

At Gulfstream Aerospace (Savannah, Georgia) I worked on custom $50+ million private and corporate jets, including one for Tom Cruise. Currently I am an associate engineer at ATK Space Systems in northern Utah. We provide propulsion systems for rockets and missiles, and aircraft flares and decoys. ATK made the two big white rockets on each side of the Space Shuttle. We also make the propulsion systems for the Minuteman Intercontinental Ballistic Missile and the Trident nuclear submarine missile.

What kinds of skills are needed for this profession?

Attention to detail, understanding of spatial relationships, and appreciation/curiosity about how things are made.

What kind of technology is needed for this profession?

Drafters will use state-of-the-art computer-aided design software to produce 3-D models and 2-D drawings. They will be expected to know the standard "Office" type suite of products. Higher-level drafters will be expected to know materials and the interaction/compatibilities of different materials.

What are the pros and cons of this profession?

Pros: Steady employment—I have not been unemployed in thirty years; interesting and challenging work assignments; can be used as a starting point for higher level design and engineering positions; you can see the results of your work—"I helped design that airplane."

Cons: Can require long hours, particularly in aerospace companies; sitting in an office environment all day long.

What is a typical day like for you in this profession?

Meet with design team to approve concepts. Create 3-D models of detail parts, arrange part models into assemblies. Create engineering drawings defining size and acceptable variations of sizes to ensure form, fit, and function of the parts and assemblies.

Certification requirements vary by state, but it's safe to say that most states (if not all) have some kind of standards that they expect their tradespeople to abide by in order to work in the industry. This protects the workers and the consumers alike. In the state of Utah, for example, many tradespeople are required to have certifications. Painters, for example, are required to pass tests for their licenses. One of the topics on their exam is chemicals, which paint is considered to be. Painters need to know about the dangers of chemicals found in their paints and varnishes and the proper way of using and disposing of them. In the state of Virginia, there are five different types of certification levels. The lowest is the Workplace Readiness Certification. The next level up is a state licensure. Just up from that is the Occupational Competency Assessment, and then the Pathway Industry Certification. Finally, the top level is the full industry certification. While these specific levels are unique to Virginia, other states have similar qualification levels that allow workers to demonstrate their competency in a particular field and skill set.

Many CTE students are actually able to obtain certification and state licensures upon finishing their coursework in the high school or college level. This allows them to move right into the workforce after graduation. In Virginia, for example, an average of three thousand students every year obtain full industry certification upon completion of their CTE programs.

Chapter Five

IN THE WORKFORCE

5

So, now you've chosen your field of interest and have finished your training. How do you go about finding work? The first step is finding the jobs. You can do so in a variety of ways: look on the Internet, go to job fairs, look on job boards, visit a state job service center, network with other people, or utilize social media.

Once you have found some job openings, you need to apply for them. Some places will just require you to fill out a job application. Others will want you to do that along with submitting a copy of your résumé. That's where some computer skills will come in handy. If that isn't your cup of tea, then initiate the help of someone who is savvy with that.

On your résumé, you will want to include your education or training and any degrees or certificates you might have. You will also want to include your employment history in the particular industry of the job for which you are applying. If this is your first job in the industry, then include other jobs that might be

Job fairs give prospective applicants a chance to introduce themselves to employers, hand out their résumé, and hopefully land an interview.

related or that can demon-strate skills in leadership and teamwork. You can include unpaid internships, work-based learning, and apprenticeships in the employment part of your résumé.

A résumé should also include your specific skills and any tools, technology, and equipment that you know how to use. For example, if you are trained to use specific heavy equipment, then include that on the résumé. If you are skilled at framing, cement work, and roofing, then most definitely include that on your résumé. You also should include inter-personal skills like your ability to work with others, your ability to lead and train others, your ability to help customers, and so forth. If you are asked to submit a résumé, you should also send along a cover letter. Essentially a cover letter is just a brief introduction of yourself and your skills. You don't need to go into too much detail; just sum up some of your top qualities and how they relate to the position for which you are applying.

Before and After the Interview

Some people feel uncomfortable talking about themselves in a résumé and cover letter. They feel like they're bragging. This isn't a time to be humble. Well, it is to some degree. You don't want to come across as arrogant in your résumé and cover letter because that definitely is unattractive. However, the prospective employer needs to know if you're the right person for the job, and you're pretty much the only person who can do that. You need to wow the employers that you are sending your résumé to! Prove to them that you'll be a good asset for their company. You know if you were hired you'd do a good job for them, but you need to convince them in your résumé and cover letter so you can move to the next step: the job interview.

There are some basic techniques to follow in a job interview. First, make sure you are dressed appropriately. Construction industry jobs require their employees to be a little more casually dressed. However, in a job interview, it's still a good idea to wear business casual attire. That would mean a nice button-down shirt and some khaki slacks for men and women. If you're applying for an office job in this industry, then more formal attire might be appropriate, such as a nice suit and tie for men and a pant suit or blouse, skirt, and blazer combo for women.

Be pleasant in your interview. Smile, look the interviewer in the eye, and be polite.

Make sure you are also well groomed. Also, be prepared for the interview by knowing about the company and the specific position. Make sure you're well fed

IN THE FIELD: DAVID DUVALL, ENVIRONMENTAL CONSULTANT

Why did you decide to go into this profession?

I enjoyed my classes at Brigham Young University in this field. I was studying to go into urban, rural, and environmental planning. Part of the program included taking some environmental classes. I ended up enjoying the environmental classes more than my planning classes so I decided to change my major. At that time I did not know what I was going to do when I finished college. Before and after I graduated, I applied for a lot of different jobs that were related to my field and posted my résumé online. I received a call one day from a company out of Texas that needed a storm water inspector in Utah, and they were wondering if I would be interested. So, I sent in my résumé, had an interview, and I got the job. I have been working in that field ever since.

What training or education did you need to have?

For my job, I needed a bachelor's degree before I would be considered for the job. I have also received additional training. I am a certified professional in erosion and sediment control. This is a certification that requires seven years of experience, training, and passing a certification test. Being a certified professional in erosion and sediment control has helped me very much with my job. There are also many other environmental certifications that are helpful.

What is a day on the job like?

Every day is a little bit different. I write storm water pollution prevention plans for construction and industrial sites. Completing these plans is a lot of computer work. I also visit construction and industrial sites to identify their needs for the pollution-prevention plans. Also, part of my job is to inspect construction sites and industrial sites to be sure that they are complying with the regulations. Another thing that I do is conduct training for construction and industrial companies. The company that I work for also has a web service that we provide. I do training for the software and support on the software. I also receive calls and answer questions about regulation issues that people are dealing with. At times, I consult with companies who have violations with the state and the EPA.

What kinds of people generally do well in this profession?

People who are good with working with other people and can communicate what needs to take place in stressful situations. Also those that like change and different things taking place each day and week: some days bring many surprises. Also people need to be good with technology. The job takes a lot of organization with all that is going on and all of the changes that can happen each day.

continued on page 64

continued from page 63

Did you take any classes in high school that helped prepare you for this profession?

I did take quite a few science classes in high school, which gave me a good background to help in college. My computer classes and math classes also helped to prepare me for college and my profession.

What advice would you have for a teen who would like to go into this profession?

Learn the different sciences. Study the environment. Decide what you want to do with an environmental degree. There are so many different environmental jobs out there. Many of the environmental jobs are specialized, so if you know what you enjoy, then learn all you can about that area. Try to get involved around your community, state, or EPA. They are all required by law to listen to public input on certain issues. There are also a lot of groups out there that you can volunteer with and learn a lot about the environment. Many cities have volunteer opportunities that can help with environmental issues within their city. The most important thing is to get a degree and be involved in an internship, or a part-time job at an environmental company (many hire college students to assist with environmental projects), or volunteer to learn more about the issues. To get a job, it always helps to have some kind of experience prior to graduating from college.

and well rested so you can think clearly and answer questions appropriately. Make sure you use appropriate language in the interview and that you smile and have a good, positive attitude throughout. At the end of the interview, thank the people for their time.

A Good Work Ethic

If you keep trying and keep applying for jobs, eventually you will find one that will work well for you. However, once you're hired, the job pursuit isn't over. You have to constantly be proving yourself to your boss and your fellow employees, that is if you want to keep your job and advance in the company. Just remember, though, that the best employees in the workforce aren't necessarily the ones with the most talent. They are more often the ones who work the hardest, are eager to learn, have a great attitude, always show up for their jobs, and keep trying no matter what. "To be a good employee, you have to be hungry for the job," James Morrison emphatically states. "You have to pay attention, learn as quick as you can, and retain as much as you can. You also must give an honest day's work. And always, always, be on time. One time that you are late can be forgiven, but twice and you can be fired. I always show up thirty to forty-five minutes early for my job and sit in my truck and think about all the things that I need to get done for the day so that I'm mentally prepared when I clock in."

This kind of work ethic is exactly what will keep you gainfully employed in any industry, but especially in the field of architecture and construction. There are many

Surveyors are essential for pre-construction planning and during the length of the construction process to make sure the building project is carried out correctly.

opportunities for advancement in this field, you just have to have the ambition to try for them and stand out from the rest of the crowd. If you do so, you'll always have work and you'll be able to move up the career ladder.

The field of architecture and construction is an exciting one with many, many possibilities. "You'll never be bored in this industry," says Sue Robinson. "There seems to always be some kind of construction going on somewhere. If you have the skills and the proper work ethic, there are many opportunities. It's all up to you."

Glossary

apprenticeship The process of working with an expert to learn a trade.

carpentry The art or technique of working with wood.

certification A document that attests to the validity of something.

commercial Of or relating to business or trade.

drafting Drawing done with the help of rulers, scales, or compasses for the purpose of specific blueprints for machinery or buildings.

excavator A person who digs into earth, gravel, or sand.

foreman A person who serves as the leader or boss of a construction crew.

framing The act, process, or manner of constructing a building.

license A document that certifies that someone can do a specific task.

mentor A person who has expert knowledge and serves as a counselor or guide.

remodel To change the structure, style, or form of something, such as a building.

résumé A document that lists a person's work and education experience for a job.

sod The surface of the ground covered by grass or turf.

technical Relating to anything that is mechanical or scientific.

truss A rigid framework made usually of wooden beams that is designed to support a structure such as a roof.

For More Information

ACE Mentor Program of America, Inc.
150 S. Washington Street, Suite 303
Falls Church, VA 22046
(703) 942-8101
Website: http://www.acementor.org
ACE reaches more than eight thousand students
   annually, making it the fastest-growing mentorship
   program in the construction industry.

American Institute of Architecture Students (AIAS)
1735 New York Avenue NW
Suite 300
Washington, DC 20006-5209
(202) 626-7472
Website: http://www.aias.org
The American Institute of Architecture Students is
   a nonprofit, student-run organization dedicated
   to providing unmatched programs, information,
   and resources on issues critical to architectural
   education.

Council of Ministers of Education, Canada
95 St. Clair Avenue West, Suite 1106
Toronto, ON M4V 1N6
Canada
(416) 962-8100
Website: http://www.cmec.ca/en
This intergovernmental body was founded in 1967 by
   ministers of education in Canada. It is meant to serve
   as a forum to discuss policy issues and consult and
   cooperate with national education organizations and
   the federal government.

CTE
8484 Georgia Avenue, Suite 320
Silver Spring, MD 20910
(301) 588-9630
Website: http://www.careertech.org
The National Association of State Directors of Career
    Technical Education Consortium represents the state
    and territory heads of secondary, postsecondary,
    and adult career technical education in the United
    States. The association's website gives information
    on career clusters, career technical education, policy
    and legislation, and other resources for career and
    technical education.

CTE Solutions: Certified Technical Education, Canada
11 Holland Avenue, Suite 100
Ottawa, ON K1Y 4S1
Canada
(613) 798-5353
Website: http://www.ctesolutions.com
This organization offers online programs for students
    in Canada. It provides courses for students to
    complete their certification, learn about a topic,
    and also gain knowledge in other career education
    topics. Courses can be taken from anywhere that
    has a reliable Internet connection.

National Association of Women in Construction (NAWIC)
327 S. Adams Street
Fort Worth, TX 76104
(800) 552-3506
Website: http://www.nawic.org

Founded by sixteen women working in the construction industry in 1953, the National Association of Women in Construction provides its members with opportunities for professional development, education, networking, leadership training, public service, and more.

Society of Women Engineers
203 N La Salle Street, Suite 1675
Chicago, IL 60601
(877) 793-4636
Website: http://www.swe.org
The Society of Women Engineers is an organization that gives women engineers a unique place and voice within the engineering industry.

Trailblazers
University of Virginia
Career Services Office
Bryant Hall, 2nd Floor
Charlottesville, VA 22904-4134
(434) 924-8900
Website: http://www.ctetrailblazers.org
The Trailblazers project focuses on labor market issues and on student courses in career technical education that can be utilized by anyone interested in CTE overall.

U.S. Department of Education, Office of Vocational and Adult Education
400 Maryland Avenue SW
Washington, DC 20202

(800) 377-8642

Website: http://www2.ed.gov/about/offices/list/ ovae/pi/cte/index.html

The Department of Education provides information on federal initiatives that promote and sustain vocational and adult education.

U.S. Department of Labor

Postal Square Building

2 Massachusetts Avenue NE

Washington, DC 20212-0001

(202) 691-5200

Website: http://www.bls.gov/ooh/home.htm

This government department provides people with in-depth information about occupations in various fields, such as pay rate, education level, on-the-job training availability, growth rate, and projected number of future jobs

Websites

Due to the changing nature of Internet links, Rosen Publishing has developed an online list of websites related to the subject of this book. This site is updated regularly. Please use this link to access the list:

http://www.rosenlinks.com/TRADE/Arch

For Further Reading

Allen, Edward, and Rob Thallon. *Fundamentals of Residential Construction.* Hoboken, NJ: John Wiley & Sons, 2011.

Becker, Holly, and Joanna Copestick. *Decorate: 1,000 Design Ideas for Every Room in Your Home.* San Francisco, CA: Chronicle Books, 2011.

Black & Decker: The Complete Guide to Plumbing. Minneapolis, MN: Creative Publishing International, 2012.

Black & Decker: The Complete Guide to Wiring, 5th Edition: Current with 2011–2013 Electrical Codes. Minneapolis, MN: Creative Publishing International, 2011.

Black & Decker: The Complete Photo Guide to Home Improvement: More than 200 Value-adding Remodeling Projects. Minneapolis, MN: Creative Publishing International, 2009.

Black & Decker: Working with Drywall. Minneapolis, MN: Creative Publishing International, 2009.

Green, Kimberly A. *The Career Pathways Effect.* Kindle edition. Cord Communications, Inc., 2013.

Hampshire, Kristen. *Black & Decker: The Complete Guide to Landscape Projects.* Minneapolis, MN: Creative Publishing International, 2010.

Kicklighter, Clois, and Walter C. Brown. *Drafting and Design.* Tinley Park, IL: Goodheart-Wilcox, 2008.

Messervy, Julie Moir. *Home Outside: Creating the Landscape You Love.* Newtown, CT: Taunton Press, 2009.

Minks, William R. *Construction Jobsite Management.* Clifton Park, NY: Cengage Learning, 2010.

Rogers, Leon. *Basic Construction Management.* Washington, DC: Builder Books, 2008.

Scott, John L., and Michelle Sarkees-Wircenski. *Overview of Career and Technical Education.* Overland Park, IL: Amer Technical Pub., 2008.

Simpson, Scot. *Complete Book of Framing: An Illustrated Guide for Residential Construction.* Hoboken, NJ: John Wiley & Sons, 2012.

Starmer, Anna. *The Color Scheme Bible: Inspirational Palettes for Designing Home Interiors.* Buffalo, NY: Firefly Books, 2012.

Tangaz, Tomris. *Interior Design Course: Principles, Practices, and Techniques for the Aspiring Designer.* New York, NY: Barron's Educational Series, 2012.

Thallon, Rob. *Graphic Guide to Frame Construction.* Newtown, CT: Taunton Press, 2009.

Wing, Charlie. *The Visual Handbook of Building and Remodeling.* Newtown, CT: Taunton Press, 2009.

Woodworking: A Step-by-Step Guide to Successful Woodworking. New York, NY: DK Publishers, 2010.

Bibliography

ACE Mentor Program of America. "The ACE Mentor Program Works!" Retrieved December 19, 2013 (http://www.acementor.org).

ACTE: Association for Career and Technical Education. "CTE Research: Fact Sheets." Retrieved December 19, 2013 (https://www.acteonline.org).

ACTE: Association for Career and Technical Education. "State Profiles." Retrieved December 19, 2013 (https://www.acteonline.org/stateprofiles).

Arrington, Barbara. Author interview, October 2013.

Bureau of Labor Statistics. "Employment Projections 2010–2020 Summary." Retrieved December 19, 2013 (http://www.bls.gov/news.release/ecopro.nr0.htm).

Byram, Thomas. Author interview, October 2013.

Calderwood, Dallas. Author interview, October 2013.

Carter, Eric. Author interview, October 2013.

Danner, Charley. Author interview, October 2013.

Dickerson, Cassy Smoot. Author interview, October 2013.

Duvall, David. Author interview, October 2013.

Duvall, Jeff. Author interview, October 2013.

Ellefson, Sandon. Author interview, October 2013.

Forbush, Zack. Author interview, October 2013.

Gneiting, Blake. Author interview, October 2013.

Howden, John. Author interview, October 2013.

Kendrick, Sarah. Author interview, October 2013.

Kern, Jim. Author interview, October 2013.

Martin, Jamie Cox. Author interview, October 2013.

Morrison, James. Author interview, October 2013.

National Research Center for Career and Technical Education. "Architecture and Construction:

Overview." Retrieved December 19, 2013 (http://www.nrccte.org).

Rask, Robert. Author interview, October 2013.

Robinson, Sue. Author interview, October 2013.

Salt Lake Community College. "Why CTE?" (Video). SLCC.edu. Retrieved December 19, 2013 (http://www.slcc.edu/cte/why-cte.aspx).

Searle, Shane. Author interview, October 2013.

State of Washington. "Career Clusters: Architecture and Construction." Retrieved December 19, 2013 (http://www.k12.wa.us/careerTechEd/clusters/ArchConst.aspx).

State of Washington. "Preparing for Your Future: Why CTE?" Retrieved December 19, 2013 (http://www.k12.wa.us/careerTechEd/WhyCTE.aspx).

Today Show. "Education Nation: CTE" (Video). Today.com. Retrieved December 19, 2013 (http://www.today.com).

U.S. Department of Education. "Career and Technical Education." Retrieved December 19, 2013 (http://www2.ed.gov/about/offices/list/ovae/pi/cte/index.html).

U.S. Department of Education. "Expanding Successful Career and Technical Education Through Career Academies." Retrieved December 19, 2013 (http://www2.ed.gov).

U.S. Department of Education. "Investing in America's Future." April 2012. Retrieved December 19, 2013 (http://www2.ed.gov).

Utah Career Technical Education. "Career and Technical Education Students Build a Home." *Utah CTE blog*. Retrieved December 19, 2013 (http://www.utahcte.org).

Utah State Office of Education. "Career and Technical Education: Giving Students the Edge." Retrieved December 19, 2013 (http://schools.utah.gov).

Virginia Department of Education. "CTE Career Clusters: Architecture and Construction." Retrieved December 19, 2013 (http://www.doe.virginia.gov).

Washington State Department of Labor and Industries. "How to Become an Apprentice." *Trades and Licensing*. Retrieved December 19, 2013 (http://www.lni.wa.gov).

Wiley, Ronnie. Author interview, October 2013.

Index

About the Author

Amie Jane Leavitt, a graduate of Brigham Young University, is an accomplished author and researcher who has written more than fifty books for young people, has contributed to online and print media, and has worked as a consultant, writer, and editor for numerous educational publishing and assessment companies. To check out a listing of Ms. Leavitt's current projects and published works, visit her website at www.amiejaneleavitt.com.

Photo Credits

Cover (figure) Ljupco Smokovski/Shutterstock.com; cover (background), pp. 1, 3 imagesolutions/Shutterstock.com; p. 5 Gilles Mingasson/Getty Images; pp. 9, 46–47 © AP Images; p. 11 Justin Sullivan/Getty Images; p. 13 Original illustration used with permission by the Association for Career and Technical Education. All rights reserved.; pp. 16–17 © Napa Valley Register/ZUMA Press; pp. 20–21 The Washington Post/Getty Images; p. 24 © Lon C. Diehl/PhotoEdit; p. 25 RJ Sangosti/The Denver Post/Getty Images; p. 30 Boarding1Now/iStock/Thinkstock; p. 32 Andrey Popov/Shutterstock.com; pp. 34–35 Lester Lefkowitz/Stone/Getty Images; p. 37 Echo/Cultura/Getty Images; p. 41 Education Images/UIG/Getty Images; pp. 44–45 Getty Images; pp. 48–49 Wavebreak Media/Thinkstock; pp. 50–51 Bloomberg/Getty Images; pp. 58–59 Spencer Platt/Getty Images; p. 61 Photo-Biotic/Photolibrary/Getty Images; p. 66 Ben Blankenburg/ iStock/Thinkstock; cover and interior elements Hitdelight/Shutterstock.com (architectural plan), Jirsak/Shutterstock.com (tablet frame), schab/Shutterstock.com (text highlighting), nikifiva/Shutterstock.com (stripe textures), Zfoto/Shutterstock.com (abstract curves); back cover graphics ramcreations/Shutterstock.com.

Designer: Michael Moy; Editor: Nicolas Croce; Photo Researcher: Amy Feinberg